7/99

UNDERSTANDING

YOUR
9 YEAR-OLD

UNDERSTANDING

YOUR
9 YEAR-OLD

Dora Lush

W
Warwick Publishing
Toronto   Los Angeles

ISBN 1-894020-09-X

Published by:
Warwick Publishing Inc., 388 King Street East, Toronto, Ontario M5V 1K2
Warwick Publishing Inc., 1424 N. Highland Avenue, Los Angeles, CA 90027

Distributed by:
Firefly Books Ltd., 3680 Victoria Park Avenue, Willowdale, Ontario M2H 3K1

First published in Great Britain in 1993 by:
Rosendale Press Ltd.
Premier House
10 Greycoat Place
London SW1P 1SB

Design: Diane Farenick

Printed and bound in Canada

CONTENTS

INTRODUCTION 9

CHAPTER 1: **YOUR NINE YEAR-OLD IN THE FAMILY** 13
Being a parent to your nine year-old - Being part of a family - When parents separate - A new baby in the family - Illness in the family - Death in the family

CHAPTER 2: **GROWING INDEPENDENCE, WIDENING INTERESTS AND UNDERSTANDING** 29
How much independence should be encouraged - Widening interests - Interest in people - Interest in sexual matters

CHAPTER 3: **YOUR NINE YEAR-OLD AT SCHOOL** 41
Learning lessons at school - Dealing with bullying - School phobia

CHAPTER 4: **YOUR NINE YEAR-OLD WITH FRIENDS AND PEER GROUP** 51
Friends are important - Cross-racial friendship - Undesirable friends - Working together with friends - Learning about relationships - Leisure activities - Conclusion

FURTHER READING 67

TAVISTOCK CLINIC

The Tavistock Clinic, London, was founded in 1920, in order to meet the needs of people whose lives had been disrupted by the First World War. Today, it is still committed to understanding people's needs though, of course, times and people have changed. Now, as well as working with adults and adolescents, the Tavistock Clinic has a large department for children and families. This offers help to parents who are finding the challenging task of bringing up their children daunting and has, therefore, a wide experience of children of all ages. It is firmly committed to early intervention in the inevitable problems that arise as children grow up, and to the view that if difficulties are caught early enough, parents are the best people to help their children with them.

Professional Staff of the Clinic were, therefore, pleased to be able to contribute to this series of books to describe the ordinary development of children, to help in spotting the growing pains and to provide ways that parents might think about their children's growth.

INTRODUCTION

It may seem artificial to divide childhood into separate years but the ages are more than convenient headings. Adults when meeting children often ask how old they are, clearly recognizing how important this is in childhood. Your nine year-old feels that nine is much more grown-up than eight but an adult of thirty-nine does not feel very different from one of thirty-eight.

The changes that we see in this middle childhood period are not as great or dramatic as those we saw in infancy or the pre-school years but nevertheless they are taking place. The average nine year-old will have developed since being eight and will develop further at ten. However, it is worth repeating what has been said in earlier books in this series, namely that the boundaries of normal development in children are wide. You may recognize some aspects of your nine year-old in this book and other aspects in the books on younger or older children.

What is specific to the nine year-old girl or boy? The age is the middle of the middle period of childhood, sometimes called the golden age of childhood. This certainly is often true as nine year-olds develop many interests, become more independent and understand much more about them selves, other people and the world, and learn many skills. Naturally, this is not the whole picture and some common difficulties of this age as well as the pleasures will be discussed.

Each nine year-old is the product of what has gone before. Many factors have combined to make your child a unique individual including that of being a girl or boy. Other factors are the genetic make-up inherited from parents and all aspects of their living conditions. Children are affected by the society they live in, the ethnic group they belong to and the make-up of their family. The care given to your nine year-old by you as parents and by other adults has facilitated intellectual and emotional development as well as physical growth. As at other ages, certain conditions, both physical and psychological are necessary to ensure healthy progress. However, the future as well as the past can influence the present. If the child and family feel reasonably secure in their environment and can look to the future with confidence, this enables the child to develop.

Encouragement or facilitation is still necessary for your nine year-old as it was at a younger age and as it will continue to be. Few children develop very well without this encouragement.

Most people nowadays do not see heredity and environment, sometimes called nature and nurture, as opposing forces but regard them as intertwining threads combining to make the individual person. Examples can be seen in families where one talent or interest predominates. Take music for instance. Certainly many musicians come from families with no obvious musical talent but many others started out from families where music was played, encouraged and was an important part of the environment.

Alison at nine was already an excellent violinist. She played in school concerts and children's festivals and had given solo performances in two public concerts. She had an older sister who was a good pianist but not as exceptional as Alison. Their parents were both professional musicians, Father being a violinist and Mother a pianist. They had noticed (being on the look-out for this) that when Alison was very young, she had loved being with them when they played, would sing and really seem to listen to the music. She started to have violin lessons when she was three years old and they praised and encouraged her. She later went to a school that specialized in music. She had other interests too but music dominated her life—to a greater extent than was the case with her sister. She talked about music, practiced without being told to do so and loved playing in concerts.

We may ask why this happened. Was Alison a musical genius, her ability inherited from her parents? Or was it that her parents had directed her towards a career in music using encouragement and suggestion rather than force? The answers probably a combination of these two views. Alison was obviously very talented or she could not have played the violin as she did at nine. But it had also entailed a great deal of work and perseverance and her personality and wish to achieve must have played an important part. Also, although her parents insisted they had not forced her, they were delighted at her musical progress and did everything possible to facilitate it.

Alison had always heard music at home and liked it. She also wanted to be like her father with whom she had a close relationship. She had always seemed to gain great pleasure in achievement and had a rather rivalrous relationship with her older sister.

Alison and her musical ability can be seen as the sum total of many factors including inherited ability, application and suitable personality, and environment, including the luck of being born into a family where her talent could be nurtured and encouraged.

Every child is unique but there are similarities between children of roughly the same age. Nine year-olds have probably not yet experienced the bodily changes of puberty and the boys do not expect to do so for some years. Girls are developing physically earlier than in previous generations but it is still unusual for girls to start menstruating at nine. The norm at this age is steady increase of height, but growth spurts may occur. Boys at nine are usually taller and heavier than girls. There are wide differences within the normal limits.

Children—especially little ones—learn a great deal by copying. They often imitate the gestures, mannerisms and ways of talking of their parents and these are then sometimes attributed to heredity, but other factors contribute to the make-up of your child. By the age of nine, your child will be very well aware that all children, like all adults, have different qualities. Some can be measured but others such as ability to get on with people, helpfulness and affection, may be less clearly definable. Sometimes it seems easy to understand your nine year-old and sometimes you may be puzzled about what is going on. No book can provide all the answers but we hope this one will give a few ideas and pose a few questions.

CHAPTER ONE

YOUR NINE YEAR-OLD IN THE FAMILY

Being a parent to your nine year-old

Being a parent can give rise to a huge range of emotions and states of mind from overwhelming happiness and fulfillment to bleak despair and disappointment. Parenting children of any age brings pleasures and problems but children of different ages have varying needs and expectations. Parents, therefore, may feel torn when trying to cater for the physical and emotional needs of children of different ages in the family. Your nine year-old may understand this but may not be pleased about it.

What is special about being a parent to a nine year-old? Much of what is true about being parent to children of any age applies to nine year-olds too. Just as every child is unique, so is every parent and every parent-child combination. Parents are different with every child even though they may set out to be the same with all of them. But all children need care and understanding. No parent is perfect and by nine your child is well aware of this. So parents should not try to live up to some fantastic standard of perfection but be aware of their faults and, when necessary, admit to the child that they made a mistake. Most nine year-olds understand the fallibility of adults and also understand that there often is room for discussion. Nevertheless, there are times when parents have to stand firm and not be swayed or worn down by arguments especially the common one that "all my class and all my friends are allowed to" stay up late, watch these videos, go out to the park alone, play outside in the early evening, and so on. Children may be relieved to have boundaries set and to see that their parents are prepared to be adults.

Being part of a group is an aspect of a necessary growing away from parental and adult domination. But your child may sometimes secretly feel that the group is going too far perhaps trouble-making or delinquency, and he or she may need to find the courage to leave the group. When parents are approachable, their children can tell them what has been happening. An easy relationship between parents and children, an atmosphere where anything and not just trouble can be discussed, makes this much more possible. Even though both parents may be working outside the home and in addition have many household tasks, finding time to talk with their child benefits everyone.

It may be necessary to forbid a dangerous activity, but a calm and reasonable approach is usually more successful than an aggressive, non-reasoning, coercive stance which only too easily evokes an aggressive response from the child. Similarly, hitting children is giving them the message that might is right and that a stronger person inflicting pain on a weaker one is an acceptable way of behaving.

It is worth considering what is the hoped-for product of successful parenting—a happy child, a healthy child, an achieving child, a happy child in a happy family—perhaps all of these.

Care must be taken not to oversimplify children's characters by labelling them. One child may be called "the good one," another "the bad one" and another "the stupid one" in the family either openly or not. These labels may constitute self-fulfilling prophecies. Each child is complex and labels only hinder understanding. The child may consciously or unconsciously try to live up to or down to this expectation and in neither case does this make for healthy development.

The uniqueness of your nine year-old also applies to her place in the family. First of all, there are variations in the material circumstances of different families. This is very obvious in world-wide terms but even within developed countries, social and income differences are enormous. Children may live in an inner city, a suburb, a small town or a village; they may live in a large house, small house, apartment or in a hostel. They may be with both birth parents, a single parent, one natural and one step-parent, with other relations and, especially in some ethnic groups, with an extended family. Children may be adopted or fostered or in care and living in a group home. They may share their lives with two separated or divorced parents, perhaps spending the week with Mother and weekends with Father. Some children of nine spend two-thirds of the year at boarding schools. This list is just a reminder of the different possible home surroundings and which the child involved considers normal.

Being part of a family

Although the traditional nuclear family is said to be less important than previously in our society, it is still the main area for emotional and social development. Children like stability and even nine year-olds, sometimes to the surprise of their parents, become upset by a change of home even if it is an improvement. However, your nine year-old can probably understand the reasons for moving when these are explained. Whatever the situation, parents have to decide how much to tell their children. Sometimes it is quite simple. At other times, parents will not want to inflict on them the burden of knowing too much. Of course, a perceptive nine year-old might have picked up a great deal of what is happening already. Children of nine will often notice an adult's preoccupation or anxiety and often (but not always) the reality will be better than the fantasy.

When she was nine Emma became very worried when she realized her parents were both unusually quiet and seemed troubled. They were less attentive to her than usual and were often short-tempered. Emma thought that her parents were going to divorce. The parents of her best friend had just separated and this friend had talked to Emma a great deal about it. Emma was an imaginative child and she was already thinking about where she would live, how sad it was to lose one parent and she wondered what would happen to their house. As well as being upset, she also had a little awareness of the power she might have in manipulating her parents. But mainly she felt upset and one day could hold it in no longer. She asked her mother if she and Daddy were going to divorce. Mother was surprised and shocked and she and Father told Emma that he had lost his job but had found another one in another district. They would have to move and they would probably have to live in a smaller house. They would have to sell their present house where they had lived ever since Emma could remember and Emma would have to go to a new school. They were now sharing quite a lot of adult anxieties with Emma. She was appropriately upset but also very relieved. She had pleasure in seeing her parents reunited in her mind but also maybe a slight tinge of regret at giving up the fantasy of living with one of them and getting presents and outings from the other. She had seen this happen to her best friend. However, Emma was mostly just happy that her parents still loved one another. She knew she would miss their house and her school friends but also felt some excitement about the coming change. She felt she could cope now that she knew they were not to be parted.

Being part of a family means learning about other people and learning to live with them. A child of nine will probably know quite a lot about the capabilities, weaknesses, personalities and roles of the different members of the family.

Each child has a special position in the family. A single mother with one child constitutes a family but makes for a very different environment from a family with far more people. Two sisters born two years apart may seem to share a similar environment but it is not the same. When Valerie, the older one is nine, her younger sister, Sylvia, is seven. When Sylvia is nine, Valerie is now eleven. Valerie can tell her younger sister what it is like to be nine. She had no older sister to do the same for her. Sylvia at nine is in a different situation from that of Valerie at nine. When Sylvia is nine, her parents have already had experience of a nine year-old and this influences them even though they realize Valerie and Sylvia are different.

Sometimes brothers and sisters get along very well with each other and sometimes they don't get along at all. Parents have to cope with this and calm the situation as much as possible. "It isn't fair" is a cry in many families. For instance Billy, who was nine, complained that Lenny who was six was allowed to do all sorts of things that he had not been allowed to do at six. These included staying up late and watching television in the evening. The parents were taken aback by Billy's complaints which they realized were mostly justified. When Billy was six, it had been more convenient to treat both him and three year-old Lenny as little boys and now they were being treated as if they were both nine. This was sorted out amicably; some changes were made in bedtimes, amount of pocket money and freedom allowed and everyone was more or less satisfied. Although Billy was jealous of Lenny's relationship with their mother and had been envious of his little-boy charm, there was also affection between them. Billy could be the helpful big brother as long as his position was acknowledged. Whether Lenny accepted this as easily is another story.

Some children with brothers and sisters are envious of only children. An only child is the focus of the parents' love, hate, pleasure, anger, hope, disappointment and ambition. This can be difficult but can be enjoyable as long as the parents realize the force of their expectations and as long as their relationship does not exclude the child. Most parents of only children make special efforts to ensure opportunities for their children to mix with other children.

An example of a difficult situation between an only child and his mother was that of Patrick. He was nine and his father had left the home three years before and had not been in touch since then. This was hardly ever mentioned but on other topics such as Patrick's responsibilities at home, they were both vociferous. The mother worked part-time and was often tired, tense and worried. When Patrick returned from school, his mother had usually just got in and she would shout at Patrick asking him to help her when all he wanted to do was slump in front of the television or play computer games. She wanted him to lay the table, empty the garbage, help with the dishes and—always—clean up his room. Patrick resisted all this and resentment flared on both sides. Possibly both were too entrenched in their positions and both were influenced by feelings which were not directly relevant to the question of helping at home. Mother saw Patrick as the embodiment of her useless, deserting husband but was not fully aware of the strength of this feeling. Patrick had enjoyed doing things with his father, although this had not happened very often, and although not fully aware of it, he rather blamed his mother for Father's departure. Until they are both more aware of the reasons behind their bitter and furious feelings and behavior, Patrick and his mother are unlikely to be able to sort out the problem of Patrick helping at home. In many other families, it can be easier than this with explanation and appeal to fairness to work out a reasonable plan. Nowadays, gender roles are not as clearly defined as before and boys are usually expected to help as much as girls.

Different ethnic groups may also have different family patterns. For example, Gurmit is a girl of nine living in a large American city whose grandparents had come from India. Both her parents were born in the United States but they kept many Indian customs. Three generations of the family lived together and other relations lived nearby.

Gurmit's mother worked outside the home but Gurmit had a very close relationship with her grandmother who indulged her a bit. She believed, probably correctly, that she was her grandmother's favorite grandchild. It was not the usual grandparent-grandchild relationship, as Grandmother did much of the caring for Gurmit, but both seemed to gain from it. Naturally, Mother sometimes may have felt a little jealous but this did not seem too serious. Gurmit, like many nine year-olds, was increasingly aware of the personalities and relationships of the adults in her family and she watched with interest, and sometimes with mixed feelings, her parents in the role of children to their own parents. Her cousins provided constant companionship but as well as the affection, there was, of course, sometimes anger, jealousy and envy. However, at school or in other situations, if one of them was attacked, insulted or even criticized, the others rushed to his or her defense.

Some children may be almost too grown-up and look after their brothers and sisters in a very responsible manner. This may sometimes be due to family circumstances such as the illness of the parents, but sometimes it is mainly due to the child's personality. Other children may be too babyish and not live up to the parents' expectations of what a nine year-old should be like.

An example of this was Fay who at nine was very shy. At school she hardly spoke to teachers or children and often acted as if she were five years old. Her father had not been at home for several years but Mother was a cheerful extrovert who loved being with people. Fay did not protest about going to school, but had little social contact with the other children there. If they played with her at all, they treated her as if she were a doll. Her written work was adequate but if the teacher tried to encourage her participation in class by asking her questions, Fay did not respond and the other children often answered for her. The school staff tried to discover what this was about. Fay had only been at that school for a year and they did not know the mother well. It emerged that Fay's mother, a loving and caring woman, was working as a babysitter, looking after several small children in her own home. It is therefore possible that Fay was acting as a small child to be minded. She was not doing so on purpose; she had told her mother she wanted to play with the other children. Subsequently the teachers and Fay's mother co-operated well and her mother tried to pay more attention to Fay and encourage her in more appropriate nine year-old interests. Fay's shy behavior did not change in a few days but the benefit of extra attention at home and more direct encouragement at school was soon obvious. Within a term, she looked more like the other nine year-olds and seemed much happier.

As family patterns in change, there are more children with half-brothers and sisters, step-brothers and sisters or both. Much is written about these relationships; the permutations of love, hate, anger, rivalries and alliances found in simpler families can be multiplied greatly in these more complex ones. A nine year-old may resent the step parent who then may feel he can do nothing right. It is easy for a child to see birth parents as totally good and step parents as totally bad but it is not always like this. Many factors affect the situation such as whether the birth mother or father is alive, whether they are in contact with the child, whether they are loving, indifferent or abusive and whether they are content, unhappy or resentful. Children usually want their birth parents to be parents rather than like friends or older brothers or sisters, but sometimes this is an easier kind of relationship for step-parents to take. If there is a great deal of tension, children often get relief by talking to someone out side the family. Many nine year-olds express themselves very well verbally and can be helped by talking about their fears, fantasies and mixed emotions to a counselor at school or a child psychotherapist, social worker or child psychologist.

When parents separate

Children whose parents are divorced or separated almost certainly nowadays know other children in the same boat and this may provide a little comfort. Sometimes, if there has been much parental conflict, it is a relief when the break comes and it makes it easier for everyone if arrangements are settled amicably. Of course, if there has been cruelty or sexual abuse, children may be pleased about the break.

Some of the conflicting feelings arising from divorce were seen in Lucy who was nine when her parents separated. She was an only child and her parents had not got along for years. They both had other relationships but had kept the marriage going "for Lucy's sake." It had affected Lucy, who was a fearful, isolated child, lacking confidence although doing well at school. Her parents tried to break the news of their separation gently. Lucy was shocked although she had been aware of their fights for years and would go to sleep pulling the duvet over her head to blot out the noise. Although she knew children of divorced parents, Lucy now worried about her future and where she would live. She had a moment of panic when she feared she would be "sent away" but she pulled herself together and listened to her parents. They explained they both loved her; she would live with Mother and stay with Father most weekends. They would all live near each other but would sell the family home so that two smaller homes could be bought. She would not have to change school. Lucy had different feelings including sadness and confusion; she wondered whether she would still see her grandparents and worried about the future of the family pets. She also wondered whether the divorce was her fault. Although not a "bad" child, she blamed herself for not always doing what her parents wanted. Her mother heard Lucy recounting her fears to her much-loved cat. Possibly she had partly wanted her mother to hear. The parents now talked to Lucy together to clear up her fears. Seeing them getting on better was encouraging to her. She was happier after their talk and gained confidence generally. Her teacher at school was supportive and she cheered up when approached by another girl in her class whose parents were divorced. They talked and became friendly and when Lucy stayed with her father, her friend often came too.

Most of the anecdotes related so far were concerned with children living with their birth parents, but many children are living with families with whom they have no blood ties, being adopted or fostered. Yet others who are taken into care live in group homes and most of these long to be part of a family. There are several different adoption patterns nowadays; adoption by a relative; adoption quite late so a nine year-old may be new to the family; adoption where contact with birth family continues. Adoption can lead to great happiness and fulfillment for parent and child but sometimes children may also have sad and bitter feelings about not belonging. Nowadays, even children who have been adopted very early are told that they are adopted, so it is rare for a nine year-old not to know. Discussion is useful although the child's natural curiosity may lead to many frank questions. Adoptive parents may sometimes be surprised at the feeling a child has about being rejected, even though they have offered explanations about the birth mother being unable to keep the baby. Usually, this is counteracted by the knowledge that their adoptive parents wanted them and love them.

A new baby in the family

It is fairly unusual for a nine year-old who has no younger brothers or sisters suddenly to be presented with a new baby in the family. But it does sometimes happen and this is how Tanya reacted. She was nine years old, doing well at school and seemed happy and popular. Then, for a few months, she seemed to be "going to pieces" as her class teacher described it. The slightest criticism or even comment on her work brought tears to her eyes and she could not summon up the competence and energy she had previously shown. Suddenly one day, Tanya said to her teacher, "My mother's had a boy. " The teacher was a little startled and said, "You mean a baby." Tanya said, "Yes, a boy." Tanya seemed less miserable now but she was still on edge and when a boy in her class spoke in the lesson, Tanya snapped at him fiercely. She did, however, soon start to become more like her old self and the teacher became less concerned about her. Tanya obviously had not, in the weeks leading up to the birth and following the birth of her brother, come to terms with being the older sister instead of the only child. She probably wondered why her parents wanted another child—did this mean they did not value her, and did they prefer boys to girls? Rational and irrational thoughts are mixed up at times like this. She may also have wondered about her parents' sexual life. She knew where babies came from but had not associated these activities with her parents.

Tanya recovered after several talks with her teacher who was perceptive and managed to find some spare time to talk to her. Tanya could then resume her place in her family as a nine year-old girl—still loved and valued even though there was a new baby who needed so much attention.

Illness in the family

Severe illness in the family imposes a strain on everyone, as in this example of a family with a mother, a father and three children, Jennie aged twelve, Graham, aged nine and William, aged six. William was ill with a chronic and potentially life-threatening illness, which left him partially physically disabled but mentally bright and needing constant attention and physiotherapy. The other two children were healthy. Graham was in a particularly difficult situation. He was three when William was born and experienced the usual jealousy but also he hoped that William would soon be a playmate. He already felt rejected by his older sister Jennie who preferred to play with her friends instead of with him. William's illness had been diagnosed soon after his birth and the work and strain of looking after him began from that time for the parents. They tried not to neglect the other children but life changed for Graham. William had periods in hospital when Mother stayed with him. Arrangements were made for Graham and Jennie to be looked after but it was not the same as having their mother there. Graham at nine years old had mixed emotions, and was more aware of them than he had been when younger. He loved William and was an exceptional brother to him. When William was well, he included him in his play and this made them both happy. He was also very sorry for William and longed for his pain and disability to be cured so that he could be like other boys. But Graham, who was a sensitive child, was also aware of less comfortable feelings including the thought that life would be easier for all of them if William died and some guilt at having a healthy body himself. Luckily, he was able to share these feelings with a school counselor who had noticed that Graham often seemed a bit too thoughtful. Once Graham realized these feelings were not wicked and that they did not destroy the positive feelings he had for William, he felt much more at ease with himself. Naturally some bitterness remained along the lines of, "why did this happen to our family?"

Death in the family

The same question of why did this happen is often around when there is a death in the family. Fortunately in the western world it is uncommon for a nine year-old to lose a parent by death; to lose a grandparent is much more common. Children often have a good relationship with grandparents and will need to go through a period of mourning and come to terms with the death. This is often the first death of someone they know well. It is sometimes harder since the parent who has lost a parent of their own will also be mourning and may not be in a fit state to help their child.

Sheila, an only child, was nine when her maternal grandmother died. Sheila had a good relationship with her grandmother who gave her presents and spent a lot of time with her. Grandfather had died before Sheila was born. Grandmother had been active until she died of a sudden heart attack. Sheila was very shocked and went through a whole gamut of emotions. First there was disbelief. Her mother said Grandmother had gone to heaven but was not very convincing as she was not sure herself if she believed this. After some thought, the parents agreed Sheila should go to the funeral as she had requested. Sheila wanted to go but she was also afraid because she had never been to a funeral before and did not even know what she feared.

The funeral was not too traumatic except that everyone cried, but later Sheila felt alone and bereft and even angry with Grandmother for leaving her. She was also angry with her mother, asking her why she had let Grandmother die. In fact, her mother and grandmother had not got along well and sometimes they vied for Sheila's love. Sheila often preferred to be with Grandmother as, unlike Grandmother, Mother had to do the "boring" things like supervising homework. But Sheila was nine and did not view it like that. Mother had not tried to break up the relationship between Grandmother and Sheila and now she was very pleased she had not done so.

Sheila soon realized that Mother was upset and felt less angry with her. Sheila now blamed herself for not doing enough for Grandmother but felt better after talking to Mother about this. The mourning period lasted some time but Sheila built up her life again and she and Mother worked at their relationship without being aware they were doing so. One day Sheila said, "People don't really die if someone remembers them and I will always have a picture of Grandma inside me." This was a comfort to her mother.

Father was very helpful to both Sheila and his wife. He was more prepared than Mother to talk to Sheila and answer questions about the meaning of death and life. Sheila asked for photos of Grandma and made a little album. Later, she became less immersed in this and she also stopped blaming herself for the death. Families may also be helped by religious beliefs. But whether religious or not, many nine year-olds are curious about death and dying, even if there has not been a recent death in the family.

The family is very important to your nine year-old; it is needed as a secure base from which to proceed towards greater maturity and independence.

CHAPTER TWO

GROWING INDEPENDENCE, WIDENING INTERESTS AND UNDERSTANDING

How much independence should be encouraged?

Childhood is like a path from total dependence to independence. This is very noticeable in your nine year-old. Children of this age often love stories about a group of children who escape adult domination and go off together without grown-ups to have adventures and fend for themselves. These books express for the children their wish and need for independence. But although the children in the books encounter many dangers, they overcome them and return safely home to the adults at the end.

In real life, having adventures is sometimes a little more complicated. Josh and his two friends, Keith and Tim, were all nine years old and wanted to go camping in a field near the suburb where they lived. This was not allowed by their parents and Josh, secretly, was a bit relieved. After discussion with all the parents, it was agreed they could camp in Josh's backyard. Everyone seemed happy with this solution, but before the camping could take place the following day, there was a very heavy thunderstorm. The rain continued the next day and the yard was flooded. More discussion took place. The adults understood the disappointment felt by the boys and could see how upset they were at the idea of postponing the camping for a week. Josh's father had an idea. Could the boys have their "camp" in the basement instead? This was just big enough and although they could not put up a tent, they could have sleeping bags. They were all pleased with this plan and it worked very well. The boys prepared some food, even raided the fridge, but when Keith suggested lighting a campfire, this was quickly rejected by the other two boys. They all joined in the pretense they were out in the wilds.

This story illustrates several points. The adults remained firm but listened to the boys and sympathized with them. The children could also listen to the adults and did not reject the idea of the basement. They showed their need for independence, adventure and fun but also realized the drawbacks to sleeping on a wet lawn. The story also shows how hard many children find it to have to wait for a treat. Keith was prepared to suggest something he knew was forbidden with good reason—a campfire—but he quickly acquiesced when the other two turned it down. The boys fantasized about where the camp "really was," they enjoyed themselves and everyone seemed pleased at the outcome.

The parents had to judge the degree of independence to allow, while assessing local conditions and hazards. Adults when reminiscing often say that when they were children they could travel around cities much more than children are usually allowed to do today. This is probably true and adults have to judge what seems sensible now. Of course, you give your children preparation and warnings. Practice in crossing roads is essential, not just learning the rules. Explanations about not going off with strangers have to take into account the child's definition of "stranger." A survey recently found that many children thought a woman or someone in uniform could not be a "stranger." Most children at nine have a sensible part of themselves which knows what to do but they also can forget and act impulsively like running across a road without looking when they spot a friend. The presence of another child can be reassuring but the two together may be more adventurous or foolhardy than one alone. Nine year-olds differ in their ability to be independent; some have to be encouraged to be more independent, whereas others have to be restrained when they suggest unsuitable outings.

For example, Marcus at nine thought he should be allowed to ride his bike alone or with a friend all over their town and into the surrounding countryside. He was skilled on his bike and knew the town well but he was impulsive and often did not stick to a plan he had made. He could tell the time but was not good at returning home at the agreed time when he was playing with friends. Marcus's parents were inclined to be impatient with him, often shouted and did not give good reasons for prohibitions. Marcus often responded by running out to friends although not actually running away. When he and his friend were planning a day out the following Saturday, a compromise was reached. His parents said that if Marcus promised to be very careful, he and his friend could go on their bikes to the nearby park and take a picnic lunch. This sounded reasonable but did not work out very well. Marcus did not return by the agreed time which had been three o'clock. By the time he returned—at five—the parents were furious and worried, had been considering going to the police, were blaming themselves but blaming Marcus more. Possibly neither Marcus nor his parents really expected him to keep to the plan but perhaps they were just tired of arguing.

Some nine year-olds need persuading even to go to the local store alone. If there is extreme fear of going out alone, some consultation may be needed. Parents' own anxieties and fantasies have to be taken into account. These must be separated from those of the child. Some parents are reluctant to have a more independent child although they might not be fully aware of this. Others may want their child to become more independent but perhaps they had traumatic events in their own childhood and are beset with anxieties which affect their judgment.

Of course, sometimes other factors as well as a child's bid for independence are around. Paul who was nearly ten said, "When I was first allowed to walk to school alone two months ago, I was very pleased and proud of myself. Now it's just boring and I would rather go in the car with Daddy like I used to."

"Boring" is a word used by children to describe almost anything negative. Is Paul getting enough of Daddy's attention at other times of the day? The ride to school was only a few minutes but it was the only time Paul and his father were alone together. Is Paul frightened of something he has not mentioned, such as bullies on the way to school? Perhaps Paul—like many adults—just prefers to ride in a car instead of walking. It should not be too difficult to sort out the real answer if Paul and his parents can talk to each other.

Growing independence is, of course, much more than being able to go around alone. It means being able to take more responsibility for yourself and is part of the growing sense of self your child is developing in relation to family, peers and the rest of the world. At nine, some children seem very organized and responsible and can remember on which days to take swimming or other gear to school, look after money for outings or relay messages between school and home. Some children never lose bits of clothing or other personal belongings. This sounds an ideal picture and many nine year-olds are not like that. At the other extreme, some children at nine seem more like five year-olds and need someone else—usually Mother acts in this role—to remember what to take and what is happening that day. But with efficient children, parents must remain the adults, even while encouraging independence. Otherwise, the over-efficient child may become too upset to seek help when it is really needed.

Nine year-olds may need encouragement to show what they can do on their own or may need to see that they are not old enough to do some things alone. Confusingly, both these responses may be needed at different times. They are no longer small children but they also are not adults in knowledge, skills or ability to understand other people and their own limitations. If they have a secure feeling that there are helpful adults around, they will be more likely to obtain assistance if necessary. Unfortunately, this secure feeling does not necessarily enable them to distinguish between helpful people and others. Many parents allow their nine year-olds more freedom in matters such as choosing their clothes, books and toys. Some mistakes will be made but intervention can stop those that are too drastic.

Shirley at nine had begun to understand a bit about family finances and what was affordable whereas her friend Eric seemed to have no idea. Shirley was, perhaps, too anxious and often seemed over-mature. Eric was not like this at all and seemed to think the grown-ups had an endless source of money and if they did not get him what he wanted, it was just them being mean. Shirley and Eric had to be helped and encouraged in quite different ways. They lived near each other and often played together and it might have been supposed that they could learn from each other. This did not happen because they were too far apart emotionally. They played board games together and even worked together making a model village but if Shirley tried to talk about her worries to Eric, they seemed to have no common ground. Shirley's anxieties were about her family finances. She understood some of what she had overheard at home and elaborated in her imagination the little that her parents had shared with her. Partly she sounded sensible, as when she was talking about the need to save, but then she became overwhelmed with anxiety. Eric seemed literally not to know what she was talking about. To him, the only interesting question was whether he was going to get the new video game he wanted which his father (unfairly he thought) said was too expensive. These children were at extreme ends of the understanding about money that most nine year-olds have. They both needed some parental help about this.

Widening interests

Your nine year-old has ever-widening interests. Even if not especially gifted in one particular field, most children are interested in many aspects of the world, including nature, science, particularly perhaps how things work, computers and the arts such as painting, music and dancing. Games and various sports are very important to them. Your nine year-old has the potential for being fascinated by history especially from the viewpoint of how people, and especially children, lived. It is sad if schools dampen these interests instead of encouraging them to flourish. All children should be given a chance to take part in musical activities, drama and art as well as sports. Much of this should take place at school but may need to be supplemented outside school. This is fine if affordable and not overdone.

Children's use of their leisure time may lead to conflict. Parents see their nine year-olds' ability to absorb new ideas and their appetite for acquiring knowledge. They may feel aggrieved when the children are not doing anything active or constructive. But children may feel tired after school. Also, most nine year-olds like television programs or comics intended for their age and, as long as this is not the only leisure activity, it does not matter. There might be conflict, however, over comics or programs that are obviously unsuitable. Parents have to be firm here and children may be relieved, since some of this violent or pornographic material can be very frightening. It is occasionally argued that children have these fantasies anyway so what harm can it do. However, to have these fantasies reinforced on television can make them seem much more real and lead to confusion between reality and imagination. It also seems to say that this is an acceptable part of the adult world.

Most children can be reasoned with about the content and quantity of their television viewing but your nine year-old can be quick to point out how much television you watch so why should they be restricted to one hour. Programs like some soap operas are not designed for nine year-olds but many boys and girls like them. They do not seem harmful and can help children understand relationships, but parents must be prepared to discuss topics that arise.

Reading is important to many children and has not been superseded by television and videos as is sometimes supposed. There is room for them all in your nine year-old's life but possibly reading needs more parental encouragement now for it to be seen as enjoyable and rewarding.

Boys and girls have many common interests at nine including idealistic wishes to help preserve endangered species or aspects of our planet, such as rainforests or oceans. They also often want to help people in distress such as victims of wars, famine, earthquakes or other disasters. Teachers understand and often encourage this wish to help and there are many fund-raising activities in and out of school in which your nine year-old may participate.

Parents have an important role to play in the development of interests. You do not need to pretend to know everything but you can help your nine year-old to find out the answers. Children are beginning to understand that some questions cannot be answered easily and some cannot be answered at all. Why are there wars? Why are people starving when there is surplus food? Television programs pose these questions, may give some answers but also raise other questions. Your nine year-old realizes that parents—and indeed people in power—do not necessarily have all the answers.

Interest in people

Nine year-olds can be very perceptive and understanding about their own personalities, those of others and relationships between people. They can be mature and sympathetic when things go wrong, although certainly not always. Both boys and girls will talk at length with their friends about other children, teachers or other adults. Their judgment of adults may be accurate, for example saying of a teacher, "She's moody today because she's so tired," or fanciful, but the interest and perception involved contribute to the child's understanding of the world. Boys and girls of nine are also attempting to understand groups as well as individuals. Boys are trying to see what is special about girls and vice versa. They are also aware of and interested in the different ethnic groups that make up society. Your nine year-old is now much more knowledgeable about what it means to be a member of a different ethnic group with different customs, family groupings, possibly another language spoken at home and also being treated as a member of a minority group by other people.

Although children may be perceptive about other people, they are not always kind. They may tease other children about any physical or personality defects, but there can be real concern for other people too. Sometimes this can be too great and children can feel burdened with guilt for something that was not their fault. Explanations of family finances, relationships, separations, divorce, serious illness or death, even if they do not have to do with the immediate family, might lead to anxiety in some nine year-olds and will often lead to further questions. Parents have to judge how much they know and how much more they should know. Just because nine year-olds talk openly about family conflicts on a television show, it does not mean they can face the same thing easily in their own family. But then this applies to adults too.

Children at nine are becoming increasingly interested in abstract ideas too, especially those relevant to justice. This is much more than the cry of "It isn't fair." They may start questioning and philosophizing in quite an adult way.

Interest in sexual matters

In this period of childhood, interest in sexual matters and human relationships is still around, although perhaps less at the forefront than earlier or later. It may seem more blatant nowadays than twenty or thirty years ago; there is certainly more open talk on sexual matters in newspapers, magazines and television. Of course, responsible parents try to ensure that nine year-olds do not see so-called "adult videos" but there is plenty of sexual material around apart from these. But even if children often seem to know more about sex now, it should not be taken for granted that they know as much as their talk suggests. Just because children joke about men having sex with women, where babies come from or condoms, it does not mean they understand very much. It is sometimes difficult for boys and girls to put together the things they make crude jokes about and the idea of a loving relationship. Even if they have had lessons at school (more common in secondary than elementary schools) on human reproduction and relationships, there is still an important role for parents to play. Children often pick up many half-truths and non-truths in the play ground from other children, and parents have to establish an atmosphere in which questions can be asked, information sought and puzzling or worrying matters discussed. Obviously this should start before your child is nine, but just because it has been discussed previously, it does not mean it has been fully taken in.

Naturally, there can be difficulties. Many children find it impossible to believe that Mommy and Daddy behaved "like that." Parents should not hide their physical affection for each other but also should try not to embarrass their children. However, it is through understanding that their parents—and other adults—have sexual love for each other that the children begin to put together the physical facts they have learned about sex and love. Some children may still be at the stage of appearing not to notice their classmates of the opposite sex. However, the fact that there are boys and girls together every day helps to make it easier for them to understand each other when they are older.

Nine year-olds have thoughts, ideas and fantasies about sexual relationships and their own bodies. This refers to children who have had a more or less normal life. Children who have been sexually abused often are obsessed with sexual matters and may be compulsive in sexual play which may be quite explicit. These children sometimes try to draw other children into their play and may sexually abuse other younger ones. Children who have been sexually abused need professional help.

Under their seemingly knowledgeable talk, the nine year-old may still be beset with anxieties. A common anxiety that may not be voiced is whether he or she will grow up to be a normal man or woman. This is often more intense in adolescence but does occur at nine. Sometimes half-understood talk about homosexuality can increase this anxiety. It may be there under the free and easy language of the playground. Mostly this is harmless but there may be the occasional child who is anxious about his sexual role and will need to talk to an adult about it.

No matter how many explanations are given, children will still have thoughts, feelings and fantasies about sex but hopefully these will not be too frightening or overwhelming. Children may be openly envious of the other sex or they may express contempt as a method of hiding envy. They may feel envious of adult sexuality and feel unsure that they will ever be lucky enough to find a loving partner. They may well be frightened of the violence so often associated with sex on television and especially in so-called "adult" videos if they see them. Or there may be some aspects of the basic "facts of life" that they find puzzling. A talk with parents, if they can be reasonably at ease, can give tremendous relief.

At nine, it is uncommon for girls to have started menstruating. However, quite a number do start while they are still at elementary school and this means there will probably be rumors and fanciful stories around. It is important that girls should know and understand about menstruation—and boys should too. Some parents can be confused when they hear all the talk nowadays about the sexual abuse of children and are frightened to show any physical affection to their children. This is obviously a great pity. In most instances, the difference between ordinary affection and abuse is very clear, but the child often shows what he or she wants. If your nine year-old pushes you away and rejects hugs or kisses, let him or her make the decision, but if it is a sudden change, it may be worth trying to find out why this has happened.

Parents should talk to their children about sexual matters when the children ask questions or it seems necessary for them to know something. Just as parents should not be too intrusive, neither should children. Not all questions about parents' personal life need to be answered. Do not be fooled by the seemingly streetwise, sophisticated talk of your nine year-old with his friends. Underneath, children are more vulnerable and unsure of themselves than they seem. A boy who talked a lot about "male and female condoms" and enjoyed shocking his parents, suddenly asked his mother, "But how do you get a girl to marry you?"

CHAPTER THREE

YOUR NINE YEAR-OLD AT SCHOOL

Children go to school for two purposes—to learn academic subjects and other skills and also to learn about social relationships. This latter aim is not on the timetable but happens through mixing with other children, having adult teachers with whom to relate, and keeping to the rules, both explicit and implicit. Your children at nine—as at other ages—can learn and achieve more and work to the best of their ability if they are happy and do not have too much anxiety or stress either at school or home.

Learning in lessons at school

What can you expect your nine year-old to be learning and achieving? In most instances, there will be a continuation of improvement in basic skills and widening knowledge of many subjects. These include history, geography and science and possibly a second or third language. Children vary enormously in their achievements in basic skills at nine. Some are fluent readers, write well and are good at spelling. These children may also understand well what they are doing in mathematics. Other children are just becoming literate and beginning to understand what they are reading and yet others have hardly begun to read and need special help. Without ability to read, progress in most other subjects is difficult so it should not be neglected. The longer children cannot read, the more they feel they will never be able to learn and they may lack confidence in other fields too. Sometimes success in another area helps improve the child's confidence generally but most schools are aware of the importance of the basic skills and hopefully can provide special help when necessary.

Schools vary in how much they think parents can help their children with their work. Hopefully teachers and parents co-operate over this whether there are learning difficulties or not. Some schools have special meetings to instruct parents in new approaches to mathematics or other subjects so that they at least know what their children are doing. It is to be hoped that school will also provide your nine year-old with an opportunity to participate in music, drama, possibly dance, drawing, painting and various sports including swimming and games. Instruction in using computers is now provided in many elementary schools.

The second main task of school is to help children in their socialization, learning about people and social skills. After the family, school is the most important sphere for learning about social relationships. Your child has many relationships at school but particularly important are those with classmates and teacher.

Parents of nine year-olds, like parents of children of different ages, need to know how their children are doing at school and show their children they are interested but not intrusive. It is often easier to see what is happening if you pick up your child from school but even if you do not do this, you can often tell at home whether children are contented or fed up or distressed. There are many reasons why nine year-olds may be upset; they may feel the teacher has been unfair, the work is too hard or they are having trouble with other children. Encourage your child to tell you what is happening and then discuss together what can be done. Children feel relieved if they know that teachers and parents are working together, like a small child who feels comforted by the picture he has of a Mommy and Daddy as a couple together.

Unfortunately, a few parents react like nine year-olds when faced with the need to go to the school to discuss something. The memories of their own schooldays bring back the feeling of being a child, helpless in the power of awe-inspiring and frightening adults. They may remember these emotions and fight against them by acting aggressively at school, seeming more like an angry child than an adult. The principals and other staff of most schools nowadays want to work with the parents and do not want to intimidate either parents or children.

Dealing with bullying

There may be a problem if your child plucks up the courage to tell you something but says it is confidential and asks you not to tell the teacher. Occasionally it may be something that you feel the teacher need not know—perhaps about friendships. But sometimes you think you cannot just leave it as in the following example.

Alana was nine when she told her mother that she had been bullied at school for over a year. Her mother had realized Alana was not very happy at school. She had often complained of a headache or a tummy ache and had not wanted to go to school. Her mother tried to encourage her but it usually ended with Alana crying and staying at home. Alana's mother had thought of going to the school about it but she had not felt she had anything definite to say. The secret that Alana told her mother was that one girl was leading the bullying but that several of the children in her class were joining in—mainly by calling her names. Her mother wondered why Alana had not said anything before. Alana hesitated before answering and her mother asked whether Alana was trying to protect her from hearing about unpleasant things and being upset. This can be a reason why a child does not confide in parents, but Alana insisted this was not the case. She whispered that the girl who was the ringleader had threatened that worse things would happen to her if she told anyone. Alana experienced great relief at having told her mother and seemed visibly happier. Her mother praised her for telling her but explained that nothing could be done unless the teachers knew about it. Alana now agreed readily that her mother could speak to her teacher. The teacher had not been aware of the bullying and there had been no previous complaints from children or parents. Action was now taken including serious talks to the whole class as well as to the main bully. In addition, Alana was told she could go to a special counselor or teacher if she was worried. The trouble did not clear up immediately but it improved enormously and Alana was much happier and, from that time, hardly ever had time off school.

Nowadays, children who are the victims of bullying may often receive help, at school or even the local child guidance clinic. However, the bullies often need help too. As with adults, not every child likes every other, but that does not mean he has to make the other child unhappy.

Teachers also may prefer some children and feel they can connect with some in their class more than others. Most teachers try to be impartial and it is important that the children think of their teacher as fair. It may be, however, that it is a lesson to be learned that life is not always fair. Children usually notice if, for example, a teacher prefers girls to boys, changes her mind, lacks confidence or dislikes another teacher. Attitudes towards teachers differ. Some children feel great affection for their teacher and sometimes this has to be hidden from the other children. Some children identify with their teacher and, consciously or unconsciously, may copy her opinions and characteristics. Most children are very appreciative of a teacher's good qualities and it can be a real blow when your child has to move to the next class and have a different teacher. Most children cope with this well although still feeling genuine regret, but a child who has experienced many losses in life already may feel the loss of the teacher severely and resent the new teacher.

There are many occasions when parents and school staff work well together both formally at parent/teacher interviews and informally in more casual encounters. It is then a pleasure to have discussions about children who are basically happy and achieving and to sort out how any improvements can be made. Many children like going to school and have many positive experiences academically and socially. One difficulty teachers have to deal with, is the child who just seems totally uninterested in what is going on in class. His interests outside school may be wide but his interest in school work can be difficult for his teacher to arouse. Sometimes with gifted children where the work seems too simple a talented teacher might manage by giving the child extra time and attention and special work. If the answer is less obvious, reasons should be sought, as children with emotional disturbances or who are having difficulties at home may show lack of concentration and interest at school.

Children at nine can see themselves in the total environment of the school and most nine year-olds are aware of how they fit in and can compare themselves with the other children. Most children feel insecure if they imagine they are different from the others. Any slight physical characteristic can be magnified in their eyes. Although children can be very concerned and helpful to others who have any disabilities, they can also be unkind and even cruel. Insults such as "four-eyes," "big ears" and much worse are common in the playground and there may be racist insults too. Teachers and parents need to work together in these circumstances and engage the children's helpful and concerned characteristics .

School phobia

Unhappiness at school can result in school phobia which is an extreme fear of going to school. It is usually easily differentiated from truancy as the school-phobic child is probably not delinquent and may want to go to school but finds it impossible. Sometimes, there is no reason for the fear that the child can explain. Professional help is usually needed although sometimes parents and teachers together can help the child return to school.

There are two main categories of reasons for school phobia. The first is to do with fear of something at school. These fears can be centered on the other children, the teachers, the work or a particular aspect of school such as physical education or having to attend school assembly. The other category of reasons is more centered on what is happening at home. Is there friction between the parents which has increased? Is there a high degree of anxiety at home? Is one parent ill or depressed?

School phobia rarely starts suddenly at nine years old without a particular reason. This reason may seem so trivial or fantastic to adults that they may not recognize it. But more commonly, if a nine year-old is frightened of school to the extent we can call phobia, then it probably has been hatching for a long time. Investigation often reveals that the child has been reluctant to go to school from the beginning.

Sometimes there may be a simple explanation which the child can give about fear of school and which makes it easier to act, but often ordinary encouragement is not enough.

George, at nine, refused to go to school and became extremely distressed if attempts were made to get him to return. Various ordinary procedures were tried unsuccessfully so George's mother took him to a child guidance clinic. One of the clinic staff tried to take George to school. This seemed to work until George was within sight of the school. He then became terrified. The attempt was soon abandoned and a child psychotherapist saw George while a social worker saw his parents. Some family interviews also took place. It emerged that there had always been difficulty in getting him to school. He had cried when his mother took him to play group so this had been quickly given up. Once he started school, George had frequent colds and always insisted on staying at home on the slightest excuse. His parents were never very insistent about school attendance. It was always more difficult to get him to return to school after a break of any sort. More recently, his father had been involved in a minor car accident, his mother was worried and his older brother was out of work. Also George's pet dog had died. This added up to a general picture of depression and illness at home. The principal at George's school was very unsympathetic to George, thought his parents were too weak and that they should just be firm with George. He said to them, "Just give him a good talking to and send him back."

At first at the clinic, George felt uncomfortable and was very wary of the child psychotherapist. His mother had forced him to come to the clinic, telling him that if he did not, he would be sent away. But George was reassured when the psychotherapist made no attempt to get him to return to school. When he came back to the clinic a week later, George was pleased to see the psychotherapist and talked to her. He realized he felt uneasy about his family and that he did not like leaving them all together at home when he was the only one going out. Later it emerged that at a deeper level George had a fantasy that his parents and brother would not be there when he returned from school. There was another hidden fear that they might all die. A little part of this was a wish to punish them for trying to force him to go to school. During several months of therapy he became more aware of his feelings and how school represented being away from his family. He was able to separate rational concern about his parents from irrational fears. It was not thought advisable for George to return to the same school when he eventually felt he could face school again. A school was found with a more sympathetic principal and George soon settled. George had needed to become aware of his fears and fantasies before he could understand that he was more worried about leaving his family at home than going to school.

Your nine year-old is developing skills and capabilities but not necessarily at the same speed as others of the same age. Children are competitive enough without this being fostered too much by adults. Areas of competitiveness apart from work include physical abilities such as sports, special skills and also possessions, including sports equipment, video games and clothes. This can be a problem in schools and the staff are generally well aware of it. Some schools try to overcome this type of competitiveness by having a uniform and not allowing expensive toys to be brought to school, thus hoping to avoid theft which can result from envy and competitiveness.

School should be enjoyable but your nine year-old may find it tiring too. A day at school for a child is like a day at work for an adult. If nine year-olds want to do nothing sometimes or just play around idly when they return from school, this is understandable as long as it does not happen all the time.

Most children attend schools which are mixed—girls and boys, socioeconomic and ethnic mix, different religions. This is an important part of education, learning to be with other children and understanding more about them.

YOUR NINE YEAR-OLD WITH FRIENDS AND PEER GROUP

Friends are important

Your nine year-old's peer group is very important to him or her. Peer group means a group of equals—in age anyway—and is not identical to a group of friends. Many children seem to live in two worlds, that of their friends and peer group and that of their family. The two worlds may blend well and inter weave without friction or may be two opposing factions. Friends are necessary to the great majority of nine year-olds. The child and friends may be regarded as a gang by the adults, suggesting they get up to activities the adults do not like. Or they may be considered a group, which suggests they have adult approval. Friends share interests, some of which seem undesirable to adults. Even if not delinquent, they can seem stupid, time-wasting, non-creative and not growth-promoting. At nine, shared activities of this nature include continual games of soccer (mostly boys) or endless video games or reading comic books (girls and boys).

Children use the word "boring" frequently, but the activities of children which are often regarded as boring by adults are not considered such by the children. The reverse also applies. Nine year-olds often think of family get-togethers as boring and attend reluctantly, sometimes only after fights, threats or bribes.

The social engagements children like usually involve their friends. Hopefully, most children of nine are used to visiting homes of other children. Going to homes of friends is a necessary part of expanding their world. This applies particularly if the friends are from a different socio-economic or cultural background. It is a pity if parents feel they have to restrict children's visits to families with a similar background to their own. Naturally, care must be taken, contacting parents and not leaving the arrangements entirely to the children. This has to be done with tact with your nine year-old. If you want to invite another child and your child disagrees, there must be a reason even if not voiced, possibly just that the two children do not like each other. Children choose friends for many reasons and friendships may arise between children with differing personalities or from different backgrounds.

Cross-racial friendship

Here is an example of cross-racial friendship. Tarjit, whose parents had come from India, was nine and had been friendly with Anita who had come to Tarjit's school at the beginning of the term. Tarjit had been to Anita's home twice and had been welcomed by her parents and the two girls had played and gossiped happily. Tarjit had rarely been in the home of a white girl, since her parents mixed mostly with other

Indians. Now she wanted to ask Anita back to her house and Anita had said she would like to be invited. What was holding Tarjit back? It was not fear of rejection, as Anita clearly wanted to visit Tarjit. It was not fear that Anita's parents would not allow her to come, as they had welcomed Tarjit to their home and seemed to approve of the friendship. It was not that her own parents disapproved of non-Indian friends.

The reason Tarjit was reluctant to invite Anita was that once before she had brought a white girl home and the girl had laughed at the Indian decor, ornaments and food. Tarjit valued her friendship with Anita and did not want to risk the same thing happening. Finally Tarjit's mother managed to talk to Tarjit about why she had not invited Anita and Tarjit voiced her fear. Her mother persuaded her to take the risk, emphasizing that if Anita laughed at their home, she was not worth having as a friend, but added that she did not think this would happen. Tarjit plucked up her courage and made the invitation. Anita was delighted and came the following week. All went well. Anita was interested in some of the ornaments, fascinated by Tarjit's collection of dolls and thought the food was similar to the food she had with her parents at the local Indian restaurant. Anita enjoyed talking, laughing and joking with Tarjit in a more intimate atmosphere than at school and appreciated knowing that Tarjit liked her.

Sometimes children may prefer being in their friends' home to their own and parents may find this rather irritating. It may happen, of course, that children have good reasons for disliking their own home. Reality is sometimes grim and children may imagine and wish that they really belonged in their friends' home. It may be that a child is very envious of a friend's possessions or family. Children who are very envious have a hard time as they are never satisfied with what they have.

53

Children may not be aware of underlying reasons why they like some children and do not want to be friends with others. When parents and children disagree strongly over the suitability of friends, the more the parents stress the undesirability of the friends, the more attractive they seem. If the parents have good reasons, these should be explained, but children are often fiercely loyal to their friends. If two friends have completely contrasting personalities, this may be helpful to both children; friends may complement each other and really enjoy each other's company and each provide what the other may lack.

Undesirable friends

However, there are times when a child does take up with another child or children who are "undesirable." Parents usually assume that the other children are the bad influence on theirs and not the other way around. Sometimes it is just that both children together get into more mischief than either would alone. There are times when parents must intervene and this may be forced on them by neighbors, teachers, social workers or even the police, any of whom might see the child—even at nine—as being out of control. A child does not always resent the intervention of parents and may even welcome it.

For example Martin was part of a gang of boys who had been enjoying themselves but whose activities were now becoming more delinquent. They were aged between nine and twelve and Martin was one of the youngest. They had broken into a shed in the local park and also had explored a couple of backyards nearby belonging to empty houses. They were now talking of getting into the houses soon and seeing if there was anything worth taking. Their activities included stealing candy from stores, smoking in the shed and they had started some sexual play with each other. Martin was becoming increasingly uneasy about this and other activities and now was not enjoying his time with the gang, but still felt some loyalty to them even though he did not like what they were doing. Martin's parents had just started being aware that Martin was uneasy about something. They realized he was unhappy and even frightened and also realized it was about the gang's activities, as he always evaded answering questions about these. Martin's parents did not know any details but understood that it was important he should not feel torn between home and gang. His parents managed to impress Martin with their wish to help and he told them enough for them to realize that he wanted to leave the gang. They remembered some of the feelings they had about friends when they were Martin's age and set about finding a solution to the problem. They told Martin he was forbidden to play outside after school or on weekends. Because this fitted in with his wishes, Martin readily agreed. He had already realized, although not in these words, that the level of violence, cruelty and degradation in the gang was growing fast and he knew he disliked it and was frightened. He was still torn a little between thankfully obeying his parents and the fear of being seen as a "sissy" by the gang. Mainly though, he welcomed the support and intervention of his parents. He may have lost face a little when explaining to his former friends that he was no longer allowed out to play but this was the preferred alternative. Martin was very reluctant, like many children, to be a snitch but his parents had found a way of helping him over this. They then had to consider whether they should take it further but could not do much without Martin's help. They felt that this should wait a bit. In the meantime, they found other things for Martin to do after school and on weekends.

Working together with friends

The children in the next example can be called a group rather than a gang. Jane and her friends, four girls of the same age, wanted to help save whales from extinction. Jane was very fond of animals like many children of nine. She soon emerged as the leader in this group. She was energetic, had many ideas and spoke with conviction, but could also listen to the opinions of others, was good-natured and kind and so she was popular. The five girls decided to form a club called "The Westlake Society to Save the Whale." (Westlake was their neighborhood.) They had long arguments about where to meet, the details of the club rules, the membership and who was to be leader. It was not automatically assumed that Jane would have this role, but after much discussion, she was chosen. They decided to meet in a shed in the grounds of the apartment block where one of the girls lived. There they spent a great deal of time writing out the rules, making badges and decided on future action. They argued over whether the club should be secret or not. Secrecy was attractive but they decided that it would be better for the cause if the club was not secret. Finally, after the club had been in existence for a month, they worked out their action towards saving the whale. The plan was not stupid. They were going to write to the government and also to some other world leaders and urge them not to kill whales. They did actually write a letter to the President and sent it. They were delighted to get a reply but then Jane became more interested in something else. She quarreled with her "best friend" who had been in the club and the club disintegrated.

There are several points of interest in this narrative. First is the genuine love of animals. Animals are often easier to love than younger sisters and brothers but it is a real altruistic feeling; secondly, the growing ability of children of this age to work together; thirdly, the developing capacity of the children to understand each others' strengths and weaknesses. Jane was the ultimate choice as leader when the realization of the usefulness of her organizing qualities overcame the envy and jealousy aroused. Another girl was chosen to do the actual writing because she had the best handwriting. Knowing where to send the letter is another indication of the growing understanding of their world. The petering out of interest and the importance of the friendships and broken friendships in the group which led to its disruption are common occurrences at this age. Although they were not aware of this, the girls were imitating adult behavior, including that on television. Their parents approved of the group although they considered it a bit of a waste of time. The girls however, were learning a great deal about working together, understanding people and committee work. One lesson they were not ready to learn was how to share all this with boys.

Learning about relationships

As at other ages, "best friends" are very important both to boys and girls. Your nine year-old can have more than one "best friend" at a time but often there is only one until a third child breaks up the original friendship. If you ask your nine year-old about her friends, she will often tell you a long story about "Mandy who used to be my best friend but then she started hanging around with Susie and I was upset but then Susie said she wanted me to be her best friend so I said 'Yes' and then Mandy was upset . . ." The ramifications seem endless and adults may take them lightly but they are the cause of much distress as well as much pleasure and excitement amongst children. A great deal of feeling enters into the relationship and even if the friendship does not last, it should not be laughed at. These friendships can last for many years and go on into adult life, but even if they are over quite quickly, children experience warmth, companionship, humor and shared interests as well as the more negative feelings of jealousy, hatred, envy and sadness.

Through their peer group, children learn about relationships, personality differences and also how different families live. Nine year-olds are developing understanding of moral issues including tug of loyalties and tolerance of other people and their weaknesses. But things do not always go smoothly; when things go wrong, prejudices, including those towards ethnic minorities, may come to the fore.

For example, Robbie, who was nine had recently changed his "best friend." He no longer played with Jimmy but now was usually with Ahmed. They shared a great interest in stamp collecting and compared and swapped stamps and talked about them for hours. Jimmy and some of the other children in the class started calling Ahmed "Paki" in the playground and insulting him in various ways with racist overtones. Ahmed was very upset but Robbie supported him and this gave him some comfort. Robbie wondered what to do and after thinking it over, he decided to tell his parents. They agreed he had done the right thing in telling them and they spoke to the class teacher. The teacher, a man, had just become aware of the trouble and had been talking to the principal about it. They decided the whole school should be addressed by the principal but that the teacher should also speak to the boys' class. The teacher did not mention Robbie, Ahmed or Jimmy by name but spoke of differences and similarities between children of different races. He pointed out the unpleasantness and stupidity of attacking people because of differences of color or anything else. He spoke well and it had an effect. The insults stopped and class discussions on the themes of tolerance and understanding others were initiated. Robbie and Ahmed were very pleased although Ahmed remained a little wary for some time. Jimmy was somewhat less delighted and still kept away from Robbie and Ahmed but the insults stopped. Jimmy eventually found other friends and the tension in the class lessened.

Children who feel reasonably secure generally will usually also feel secure in their peer group and this helps towards being accepted and popular. But other factors are also important such as the nature of the group and how much the child wants to be popular. Some children may achieve popularity on the basis of being anti-parent and this may be quite complicated since it's possible the child can only be so anti-parent because of feeling secure at home. In other instances, the rebelliousness is more permanent and more bitter. Some children do not have to court popularity and some do not seem to care whether they are popular or not.

Parents sometimes know little about their children's friendships and sometimes do not like what they see. It may be easier for adults to see the negative side of the peer group than the positive. Children are often helpful, comforting and caring with each other and also have a lot of fun. Children say friends stop them being "bored" which is always seen as something to be feared. Learning about friendships is an important developmental step as the following examples illustrate.

Steven was very pleased with his new personal stereo. He lived in a rather rough area in an inner city but prided himself on being "street-wise" though he was only nine years old. He and his friend Gerry were playing with the personal stereo one day in Steven's apartment when he suggested going to the local park. Both boys knew it was not very wise to take the personal stereo to the park but they egged each other on. In the park, they were attacked in a quiet spot by two older boys who did not really hurt them but stole the stereo and ran away with it. Steven had desperately tried to fight the boys but Gerry had run away very quickly. Gerry returned when the attackers had vanished and Steven and Gerry went to the police station together. Both were very upset. The police said there was little they could do. Steven was then very angry with Gerry for running away but Gerry indignantly said he had gone for help. In fact, the way he had returned when he saw the big boys run off suggested this was not true but he may have half-believed it himself. It was the end of the friendship. Steven could never forgive Gerry for his cowardly and disloyal behavior and kept repeating to his mother that Gerry did not understand the meaning of friendship. Perhaps Steven also could not understand the meaning of friendship which could include tolerance of his friend's weaknesses. The story did not end there. Gerry was so cross with Steven—and possibly also with himself—that he related the story at school but saying that Steven had run away and that he had stayed to fight. Needless to say, this did nothing towards mending the friendship. We can also wonder why Steven took the stereo to the park. Partly, he wanted to show himself as strong and a dare-devil, as he liked this image of himself, and he also wanted to show off to Gerry.

The second example is that of Pamela who had been "best friends" with Irene for over a year. Then a new girl, Sasha, came to the school, quite an unusual occurrence in this elementary school. Sasha was lively and outgoing and managed to fit in with the academic and social life of the class quite easily. Sasha soon started playing with Pamela and Irene, and at first this worked well. Pamela and Irene enjoyed telling Sasha the school rules and customs (sometimes embroidered or exaggerated) and a lot of gossip about other children and the teachers. Almost imperceptibly, Sasha began to show preference for Irene and soon Pamela began to feel like the outsider in the threesome. Pamela lived with her grandparents and she managed to tell her grandmother about it but her grandmother did not realize its importance to her. She just told Pamela it was "too bad" and said she would soon find another friend. Grandmother added that Pamela and the other two could probably play nicely together. Grandmother was not taking into account that it is often hard to maintain three-person relationships and also that, since the loss of her parents in an accident, Pamela found it hard to bear any loss. The situation at school became more and more unhappy for Pamela and, like Steven in the earlier story, she started thinking about the meaning of friendship. She thought bitterly about how everyone had let her down. She included in this her grandmother who did not understand and her parents who had died. Soon Sasha moved on to new friends—possibly because she had already moved home a few times, she could not sustain friendships for long. Irene was now left alone and tried to return to play with Pamela. But Pamela meanwhile had gained emotional strength since her grandfather had noticed she was upset and had started talking more to her about friendship and other subjects. The warmth of this relationship helped Pamela to find new friends at school. She did not reject Irene but neither were they as intimate as they had been before. Pamela had learned something from this episode—about herself and about the possibility of making new relationships.

Leisure activities

The many leisure activities of nine year-olds have been mentioned already. Although your nine year-old may some times seem serious and idealistic, play is still a vital part of his or her life. Play is for enjoyment but also, although not as obviously as in pre-school children, it is a way of learning about the world. The range of play, games and other leisure activities enjoyed by nine year-olds is very wide but depends, naturally, on what is available in the child's environment. Some activities are on the border between play and formal learning such as taking lessons in swimming or riding. Just because an activity is organized it does not mean that it must count as work and not play. Group pursuits such as Cubs, Brownies, 4H and similar organizations and summer camps can be both enjoyable and useful learning experiences. Many children love taking part in adventures and also love the novelty, different surroundings and way of life which summer camp holidays entail. Even though the actual danger should be non-existent, children can still be thrilled by mastery of new skills and encountering new challenges. They mostly love recounting narratives of their adventures when they return. Nowadays, there are many summer camps catering for children, and for many children they are a good idea. However, they may not suit all children and it is worth discussing it with them first. You have to judge whether they only need encouragement, whether they are really not ready to go away on holiday alone or whether they are not interested in what the camp offers. If they are very enthusiastic about going, advantages and disadvantages should be discussed realistically too.

Many nine year-olds love exploring but, sadly, opportunities for doing so seem to be diminishing especially in urban areas. The idea of danger is often fascinating to both sexes although possibly more to boys than girls. Some children will be attracted by anything forbidden or supposedly dangerous and feel a need to test themselves. Children often have a talent for getting into places where they are not supposed to be; it may seem to adults that nothing is child-proof and this may lead to real danger. Hopefully children can use their love of exploring and physical skills such as climbing, running or swimming without endangering themselves if some activities are organized for them.

Baseball is still the most popular game played in the playground and boys and girls now often play together. Girls and boys are sometimes attracted to each others' toys or games. It seems acceptable in our society for boys to play with dolls as long as these are dressed for combat or "action" and it is still mostly acceptable for girls to be considered "tomboys." To many people, however, the concept of special games or toys for one sex only is outdated.

Whether in baseball, other ball games, skipping games or some current fad, interest in the rules of the game is a characteristic of this age when children are realizing that rules can be changed. When ball games have to be modified because of playground conditions, there can be long arguments about changing the rules. But when playing board games, adherence to the rules is usually seen as a necessity. Board games of all sorts are popular at nine including Sorry, Snakes and Ladders, variations on these, checkers, chess, Monopoly, word games and quiz games. Crazes rush through schools and neighborhoods like wildfire. Sometimes they are cheap like Hula Hoops some years ago and sometimes expensive, like the currently popular video games. They become part of the nine year-old culture.

Some nine year-olds can do much more with computers than just play games and some love making things with construction sets of various sorts or sew, knit or use other practical skills with or without special kits. Hobbies can grow out of first attempts at, for example, making model airplanes or doing jigsaws or other types of puzzle. There are many hobbies which attract nine year-olds and are often shared with friends. Typical of this age is the wish to collect things. The list of things which can be collected by nine year-olds is endless, ranging from fairly usual items like stamps, coins, sports cards, models (either home-made or bought), comics, books in a series, dolls to unusual items which no one else collects. Many nine year-olds love making up collections of photos or other pictures in scrapbooks and sometimes do this extremely well.

Girls of nine still play with dolls, and stuffed animals are still around, played with or used by children of both sexes, especially if unhappy or distressed by something. Sometimes this may be regarded as babyish either by your nine year-old or others, but it may be helpful and even necessary.

Games played with other children may include rituals and rhymes. Rhymes used in skipping or counting have been handed down through the ages with the original meaning lost. Sometimes, the play on words is still recognizable and this is enjoyed by nine year-olds. They love playing with words, riddles, puns, purposely misunderstanding words and changing the meanings and the words in songs and poems. This leads to almost helpless laughter but is, although not obvious to the children, a way of learning about language. The jokes around the changes of words and puns are sometimes about body functions or sex but not usually obscene. Jeers and insults are usually considered funny rather than upsetting by the children although perhaps not by the adults. They may have felt birthday parties were not enhanced by the singing of "Happy birthday to you, you live in a zoo . . ." by the guests but most birthday hosts do not seem to mind.

Dramatic fantasy play is still popular at nine. Cops and robbers and the many variations are still played. The same basic principles apply even if the groups are called spacemen and aliens. Probably these games are more popular with boys than girls. There is plenty of scope in these games, as in so many invented by children, for the fertile imagination of nine year-olds to flourish.

Conclusion

Some sad or troubled situations involving nine year-olds have been described in this book as well as many that are more cheerful. All these illustrate some aspects of children of this age and help us to understand them. Hopefully your nine year-old will not encounter too many difficulties in the year leading to the tenth birthday and entry into double figures—often seen by children as really important. The year from nine to ten should be a year of development—physical, intellectual, emotional and social and also a year in which nine year-olds and their parents enjoy themselves.

FURTHER READING

Human Development: An Introduction to the Psychodynamics of Growth, Maturity and Ageing, Eric Rayner, Allen and Unwin, London 1978
My Mom Needs Me. Helping Children with Ill or Disabled Parents, Julia Segal and John Simkins, Penguin Books, Middlesex, 1993
The People in the Playground, Peter and Iona Opie, Oxford NUP, 1993
Narratives of Love and Loss. Studies in Modern Children's Fiction, Margaret and Michael Rustin, Verso, London, 1987

THE AUTHOR

Dora Lush is a consultant child psychotherapist in the Child and Family Department of the Tavistock Clinic. She gained B.A. Hons and Ph.D. in Psychology from London University and worked as a clinical psychologist before training as a child psychotherapist at the Tavistock Clinic. She worked in a local authority child guidance clinic and then at the Child Guidance Training Center which then merged with the Tavistock Clinic. She has published papers on child psychotherapy and, for the last few years, has been involved in research concerned with how children who are adopted, fostered or in care, respond to psychotherapy. Dora Lush is married and has two grown-up sons.

UNDERSTANDING YOUR CHILD
TITLES IN THIS SERIES

UNDERSTANDING YOUR BABY	by Lisa Miller
UNDERSTANDING YOUR 1 YEAR-OLD	by Deborah Steiner
UNDERSTANDING YOUR 2 YEAR-OLD	by Susan Reid
UNDERSTANDING YOUR 3 YEAR-OLD	by Judith Trowell
UNDERSTANDING YOUR 4 YEAR-OLD	by Lisa Miller
UNDERSTANDING YOUR 5 YEAR-OLD	by Lesley Holditch
UNDERSTANDING YOUR 6 YEAR-OLD	by Deborah Steiner
UNDERSTANDING YOUR 7 YEAR-OLD	by Elsie Osborne
UNDERSTANDING YOUR 8 YEAR-OLD	by Lisa Miller
UNDERSTANDING YOUR 9 YEAR-OLD	by Dora Lush
UNDERSTANDING YOUR 10 YEAR-OLD	by Jonathan Bradley
UNDERSTANDING YOUR 11 YEAR-OLD	by Eileen Orford
UNDERSTANDING YOUR 12-14 YEAR-OLDS	by Margot Waddell
UNDERSTANDING YOUR 15-17 YEAR-OLDS	by Jonathan Bradley & Hélène Dubinsky
UNDERSTANDING YOUR 18-20 YEAR-OLDS	by Gianna Williams
UNDERSTANDING YOUR HANDICAPPED CHILD	by Valerie Sinason

Price per volume: $8.95 + $2.00 for shipping and handling

Please send your name, address and total amount to:

WARWICK PUBLISHING INC.
388 KING STREET WEST • SUITE 111
TORONTO, ONTARIO M5V 1K2